Geordie's Sea Journal

The poetic chronicles of Nevil -

a crew member on British Dry Cargo (mini bulk) ships

plying the European trade - with other contributions

from his seafaring colleagues.

Best. Wishes to
Roger Scott.

Calum. McKenzie

First published in 1998 in Britain by
Calum McKenzie, Freepost SCO2372, Port Charlotte,
Isle of Islay PA48 7BR

© Calum McKenzie Crum 1997

Designed by Gardiner Russell, Glasgow

Printed by
The Image and Print Group, Glasgow

This book is dedicated to Brenda
a sailor's sweetheart

Geordie's Sea Journal

Contents

The Poems

The author has the greatest acknowledgement to

R. Lapthorn & Company Ltd

The company was incorporated in 1954. It specialises in the provision of a complete
and comprehensive ship management service. It operates a fleet of coastal vessels built to its
own specifications. At present the company is the market leader with the largest coastal
fleet sailing under the British flag.

The author joined them in 1991, and has been pleased to draw material
from their skilled crews and prudent management team. Eddy the cartoonist,
is a Lapthorne employee and depicts a typical coaster crew
in the cartoons.

Nevil is mythical, and could be any one of these seafarers who always seems to
be the leading character of the crew.

An introduction to Nevil

Nevil was born in the North East in 1941. He was educated at a
secondary school leaving without qualifications when he was fifteen. He started work
the day after he left school as a tea boy, in a well known North East shipyard, where he was
to serve his apprenticeship as a mechanical fitter. In order to avoid National Service he
joined the Merchant Navy as junior fifth engineer. Nevil did not realise that by this time
National Service was to be over, so after one trip he continued his seagoing
profession on smaller ships mainly working to and from the Baltic,
without gaining any qualifications.

This mythical rascal seems to survive on his character alone, while always
seeming to be a crew member on the ship that his longstanding, and long-suffering
Captain McK, has command.

The Author pays special thanks to

Edward Kirkbride of Berwick on Tweed for contributing the cartoons and joke,
Dorothy Mitchell Smith for proof reading and to Patricia Lenton Halsall
for her generous support and assistance.

The Poems

When a sailor comes home from the sea

When a sailor's due home from sea,
His loved ones show great bouts
of glee.
His wife and his children,
Can't wait for the time when,
That sailor's due home from the sea.

When a sailor comes home from the sea,
His loved ones, are the whole family.
He's made to feel king,
As bells he will ring.
When a sailor comes home from the sea.

When a sailor's been home from the sea,
It starts with the apathy.
His loved ones once adoring,
Now find him rather boring.
When a sailor's been home from the sea.

When a sailor's still home from the seas,
His loved ones are down on their knees.
They're praying to God,
To ship out the old clod.
When a sailor's still home from the sea.

When a sailor's due back from the sea,
There's thanks for an answer plea.
His loved ones forget,
In time they'll regret.
When a sailor's due back to sea.

When a sailor is back at sea,
His loved ones are left on the quay.
They're sad in their heart,
At the old salt's depart.
How they long for that sailor,
To come back from the sea.

Calum McK

The Ice Bound Port of Stralsund

We loaded ferts in Antwerp, BASF was the place.
The destination Stralsund; what problems we were to face.
Hogmanay off Tershelling, that is a Friesian Isle.
The ice reports were coming, they did not make us smile.
By Kiel canal it was certain, that Stralsund port was closed.
To Rostock we diverted, this ice-free port proposed.
But NO we had to journey, to the ice of Rougen Isle.
To board the Stralsund pilot, off station fifteen miles.
The pilot boards us promptly, at first light of the day.
The plans laid out before us, we were to have no say.
We steamed towards the channel, following a larger ship.
Just inside the fairway, the ice began to grip.
The airways they were bristling, with plans to get us through.
An ice breaker sent towards us, and a tug to pull us too.
The breaker was a giant, sailed off to work elsewhere.
The tugboat it was puny; the contest was unfair.
The discussions never ending, the one thing though was clear.
The icebound port of Stralsund, we'd get nowhere near.
Now finally they accepted, Stralsund's out of play.
Diverting us to Walgast, secured by the end of the day.
Two days they're discharging, then off through thinning ice.
To Landskrona we are destined; a place I thought quite nice.

Nevil

This corner of Tiree

One night the *Maple*, came sailing through the Scaw.
   She did not know at this time, what drama lay before.
   She'd loaded at Landskrona, thirteen hundred tonnes and more.
Bound for the Port of Runcorn, that's where the cargo was for.

The captain's named Mckenzie, a noble Scot by heart.
   He didn't know at this time, how fate would play a part.
He thought about his options, what passage would he make?
   North through the rugged Pentland, or South via Dover take.

He listened to every broadcast, he studied wind and sky.
   The storms were to the southwards, and that's the reason why.
It was off the tip of Norway, that fateful change of course.
   To turn the ship for Scotland, and fill him with remorse.

She ran before the tempest, the wind was in East.
   That ship she did her damnedest, making seven knots at least.
When Duncansby was sighted, she knew the lee was soon.
   The inner sound was taken and cleared before the moon.

Cape Wrath was now well rounded and at a good old pace.
   Down through the Northern Minches, she continued to make a trace.
By afternoon of Friday, Niesh Point had passed abeam.
   Where Bert the Mate, set course for fate, to pass the rocks unseen.

The captain's watch nigh over, had he steered the course? or least,
   Had wind and tide stood side by side, to set the *Maple* East?
There was a mighty tremor, a lurch to starboard too.
   The captain stared in horror, as those rocks came into view.

He thrust astern the engines, to wrench her from the grave.
   Please God be forgiving, for this ship he has to save.
The Cape Verdi boys were awoken, to man the emergency pumps.
   It was not long after, they're back in there pineapple chunks.

The *Maple* she did answer, to engine and to thrust.
   So the course was altered, to Ireland was a must.
But Ireland could not take her, there were no facilities.
   To Campbeltown diverted, to stop those ingress seas.

The *Maple's* head was heavy, on that Saturday morn.
    The coastguards did anguish, about a coming storm.
The bow sank ever deeper, it had never been so low.
    Great seas washed over the hatches, Oh! what a bitter blow.

Then the straw was sighted, it briefly brought some glee.
    A safe anchorage in Loch Indaal, that would give a lee.
The Coastguard now could action, those hearty men afloat.
    The men that never fail you; the *men of the Islay lifeboat.*

A chopper stood at Prestwick, its crew on ready too.
    Its vital cargo loaded, this salvage pump should do.
She rounded the Rinns of Islay, and up the loch did creep.
    Would it be, Oh! could it be, he'd saved her from the deep.

Northwards to the anchorage, as winch man drops from above.
    Rescue one seven seven, was flown as if a dove.
On Bruichladdich pier they mustered, with mighty pump and pipe.
    The fire fighters of Islay, would conquer without a gripe.

Alas these pumps were puny,
Against the ragged breach.
A crew on the *Helmut Schroder*,
Called 'put her on the beach'.
There was a great discussion,
About this sandy seat.
But what about Bruichladdich,
She'd lie there pretty neat.
To Bruichladdich pier she headed,
Police Sergeant MacLean's in charge.
And many men from the Lochindaal Inn,
Had come to help that barge.
Now the ship is moored,
And the crew can take some rest.
They had yet to find out,
That they were among the *best.*

As Captain Mck reflected, about the Hebridean sea,
It's not soft sand that maketh *this corner of Tiree.*

Nevil

Maple

Sunday dawns as easterly gales blow,
Graham and his divers descend below.
They report a terrible bash,
Spreading tarpaulins over the gash.
They can't see as far as they reach,
They manage to cover that ragged breach.
I thank them all for the sterling work,
What a job in that ice-cold murk.

Now Neilan and pals of the fire team,
Work their pumps and success is seen.
In not more than half an hour,
The tanks are dry; that's some power.
The pumps on board can take the strain.
As these tanks need a constant drain.
Day and night the pumps are working,
This is no time for any shirking.

Monday morn, what tranquillity,
Seeking the best of facility.
Into the tanks like the busiest of bees,
Trying to stem those ingress seas.
The pumps are worked by a Cummings and a Lister,
How magnificent the ever-changing vista.
Now as day makes way for night,
Experts will be on the morning flight.

By Tuesday lunch there're experts three,
A director, an insurer and Ken, from class society.
Before we depart the breach we must close,
Just quite how the discussion flows
To close the breach with a welded box,
Then to the Clyde and a graving docks.
But what about now? Where's some plate?
Davie has the answer; it turns out great.

From the closed distillery an old grain hopper,
Shaped by flame there is no cropper.
The pieces made small to pass through a hatch,
Welded to beams all forming a patch.
Two welders from Goole, came by van,
Loaded right down, including a fan.
They'd driven all night across the border,
To put the *Maple* back in order.

On Wednesday night, there was a disaster.
The pumps were stopped. By the master?
No one knows who did this act,
Misconduct suspected and that's a fact.
Shaping and welding all of Thursday,
From Friday morn on board they'll stay.
Working all night past Saturday's dawn,
They've worked so long they're really worn.

I'd heard of the ceilidh; I'd give it a miss,
To sail in the morning how that would be bliss.
The charity do for a local in need,
A motorbike accident; he's now paraplege.
But Linda, the barmaid, dragged me to bus,
I had to go, or cause a great fuss.
Where in the Rinns Hall I Scottish danced.
I there met a lassie; how life she's enhanced.

Well after dawn when I board my ship,
The surveyor's inspecting before we can slip.
In these professionals we place much trust,
For the ship to be safe, to Ken it's a must.
A last-minute hitch, but not a great blow,
As condition on class to the Clyde we must go.
The diver sent down to peel off the tarps,
The ropes now slipped and the *Maple* departs.

Out of Loch Indaal and into the lane.
Close past her house my heart fills with pain.
To the dry dock at Gourock for further repair,
Then on to Runcorn in utter despair.
After discharge of cargo we wait for a lull.
Without you beside me how my life is dull.
Then round to the Medway for full reparation.
The dockyard at Chatham has good reputation.

Nevil

Tern

That Saturday morn when I left our abode,
My heart sank under a terrible load.
With Susan a lift to that damned early boat,
Once on board my heart would not float.

A lift to Glasgow with a man called Jim,
Id have turned at his slightest whim.
Now on a train destined for York,
But for my children I would balk.

On Sunday the christening brought light to my heart.
Alas on Monday I wanted to dart.
Not to Kings Lynn, where my vessel is moored,
But to the Rinns where my heart is lured.

That night I visit a few of my haunts,
And from my pals I took all their taunts.
Strolled to the Bentick with Pauline I chat.
Back to the ship I'm feeling quite flat.

On Tuesday we sailed to Boston Lincs.
Oh! how my heart, it really sinks.
Loading for Antwerp a full cargo of malt.
How I wish I'm rusty old salt.

Friday at Antwerp we discharge and re-load.
A cargo of ferts with an IMCO code.
Bound for Killingholm, a creek on the Humber.
Always aware I must make no blunder.

A Sunday pub lunch with Angie and kids,
Lifted my heart from off of its skids.
Monday's discharge came to a stop,
when afternoon rain around us plop.

So off to the pub after Coronation Street.
This extra night in a bit of a treat.
On Tuesday we sail on a falling tide.
Sped by the ebb we washed out inside.

Off to Ostend for yet more ferts.
 Oh! when you speak how my heart hurts.
Slow was the passage as lock gates are down.
 Berthing on Thursday, five miles from the town.

Loading was started as soon as we're fast.
 Not until Friday cargo finished at last.
So we depart in moderate seas.
 Destined for Middlesborough, that's on the Tees.

Now I have called on my mobile phone,
 Life is back in my every bone.
I think of the time that we'll be together,
 Hoping that's soon and for ever and ever.

Nevil

Tern (continued)

May twenty ninth
    Discharged on the Tees.
   Sailing for Lowestoft
    In more than a breeze.
Bound for a mill
    On the Brussels canal.
Ruisbrook the place
    With a visiting pal.

Jerry his name
    he a ship's chandler
A Glaswegian by birth
    And a great wangler.
Off to his house
    Greeting family.
Then back to the ship
    And reality.

On Friday we sailed
    Out of the Schelt.
Up the Dutch Coast
    We're not hell bent.
To a Europort Pier
    We make our way.
Not to be loaded
    Till early Monday.

My Sunday lunch
    At the Swiss Chalet pub.
Downing two pints
    And having some grub.
Monday we're loaded
    For New Holland Pier.
Once in the Humber
    I'd hold back a tear.

The mate's packed his bags
    He's off on his leave.
Tim Collom reports
    He nearly gave grief.
Slipped on the deck
    As he straddled on board.
He's gripping the wire
    As we heave him inboard.

One of the sailors
    gets a rope round a prop.
The DoTI boat's launched
    In that muddy chop.
Cutting and sawing,
    For over an hour.
With the task finished
    I'm straight in the shower.

While I am in there
    Having my soak.
One of the Verdi boys,
    Caused a joke.
Brad paid a visit
    He'd called from the quay.
Misunderstanding he left
    Not seeing me.

The ship was laid off
    to board was a fear.
He called to the lad
    'Tell captain I'm here.'
The guy spoke English
    That's not so good.
Brad's understanding
    The best he could.

'Cap show' was taken
    As the captain's ashore.
He left without boarding
    There will be times more.

Discharged and loaded
    At the same place.
Bound for Brussels
    but we did not race.

While anchored in the Hawk
    Awaiting the weather.
When phoning you
    My heart turns to feather.
Late Friday night
    We could made our start.
As once again
    you gave me heart.

Rolled by the swell
    From an easterly gale.
Down through the race
    She's setting a trail.
Now off Great Yarmouth
    The sea is quite slight.
Across to the Stienbank
    During the night.

Taking no pilot
    We pass up the Schelt.
The captain, he's told me,
    He'll pocket some gelt.
Onwards to Whintham,
    Here pilot is must.
But Tao's the man,
    That you can trust.

That Sunday night
    In Brussels town centre.
Talking with Tim
    He's quite a mentor.

How we got back
    None of us knows.
Tim said my directions
    Were right on the nose.

Monday's discharge
    Went all through the night,
Then back to Wintham
    and Tao's delight.
Onto the Schelt
    No pilot on board.
The captain I'm sure
    Is making a hoard.

Passing through Antwerp
    to the Rhine waterway.
This way to Rotters
    We're there in the day.
Berthing at Schiedam
    Later that night.
Strolled to a bar
    The drinking was slight.

Then when I rang
    My heart stood still.
For not to come rushing
    Took all of my will.
Thursday's a holiday
    So no work this day.
Friday we're loaded
    and sped on our way.

To Selby, an abbey town
    Set on the Ouse.
It's where I'm to leave
    With no time to lose.
Oh! how I hope
    That I will see you.
To hold you and kiss you
    Be it moments few.

Nevil

Privileged

I feel a very privileged person,
    To have witnessed a Hebridean wake.
This for a Portnahaven lady,
    The sort that they no longer make.
Borne on this Hebridean Island,
    Then left to train as a nurse.
She tended many casualties,
    As the war got worse.
After marrying a craftsman shipwright,
    She returned to this fair isle.
To practise her midwifery,
    With compassion and a smile.

This storm-raged, stone-built chapel,
    By Telford it was built.
A piper sits quite sombre,
    Resplendent in his kilt.
Through bleached timber doors we enter,
    The bearers sit to the right.
The simple rugged woodwork,
    Neatly painted white.
She lies before the pulpit,
    Steep steps for the minister to climb.
Sweet music from the organ,
    The airs are quite sublime.

Four daughters sit behind her,
    They're holding back a tear.
The mouners listen in silence,
    As the minister speaks so clear.
The service now completed.
    As bearers heed their call.
She starts her final journey,
    From beside the dry stone wall.
With Atlantic breaker raging,
    Out beyond Orsey Isle.
It's tranquil at Portnahaven,
    As the storm abates a while.

The piper heads the cortege.
    As up the brae they start.
Only the men folk follow,
    The women will watch her depart.
To the ancient grounds of Nerabus,
    Is where this lady will rest.
A stunning seascape vista,
    As she ascends, to join the best.
Around the grave they cluster.
    A dram to give them heart.
A bite of cheese is traditional,
    As they say their last depart.

Calum McK

Finch

When I left the *Tern* in the East Yorkshire Ouse.
My heart filled, with a bout of the blues.
I was not bound for my love on the Rinns.
But to the *Finch*, to purge my sins.
A few days in York with my family,
Is no compensation for being with thee.
So Saturday morn a train to Kings Lynn.
I tried on the lotto but did not win.

As midnight came we depart.
Sailing to Immingham with you in my heart.
Here we loaded Petroleum Coke.
No time to see any Humberside folk.
This is one port that they do not dally.
Sailing in hours for the Port of Calais.
Passage south was a bit of a bind.
The swell's from the north and a little unkind.

Bank holiday dawn saw the Norfolk coast.
No one on this beach was going to roast.
Midday we started across the Thames.
White tips of waves, glistening like gems.
By late afternoon we're on Calais approach,
When two in-bound ferries came close to a broach.
The English captain reporting the French.
For chopping him up in this narrow trench.

All fast and finished by nine of the clock.
I was the first away from the dock.
Off to a haunt, the Cafe Au Retour Du Ferry.
The first time I sang Karaoke so merry
'Rawhide' the number as the mike came to me.
But one of Sinatra's gave me glee.
Deep from my heart I croaked out the tune.
Hoping we're together pretty damn soon.

Calais to Barking should be no slog.
        Alas we encountered really dense fog.
Across the lanes with the fo'c's'le unseen.
        The captain is studying blips on the screen.
The radar was faulty; it took all his skill.
        I think that it gave him quite a thrill.
Passing the Goodwins, land came into sight.
        I don't mind telling, what a delight.

Westward to sea reach anchored in the Oze,
        Awaiting a pilot, but the master knows.
He's been up and down since a lad in his teens.
        This was the first time with pilot it seems.
Anchor aweigh with pilot on board.
        Only to Gravesend this professional co-ords.
Anchored again in Gravesend Reach.
        We are too early; we see too much beach.

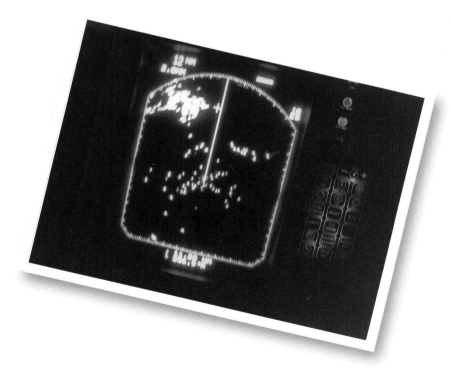

One hour more at anchor we lay.
  Then with changed pilot we're back under way.
Inwards past Tilbury and Fords so sleek.
  Through the flood barrier and into the creek.
Swinging her easy before the berth.
  Skilful manoeuvres or she'll foul on earth.
Now making fast port side too.
  The crane starts swinging in moments few.

On with the business then cap's off ashore.
  Into the City he does not adore.
Back to the ship for his evening meal.
  Watching TV with the heat unreal.
Back to the shore for a telephone chat.
  Talking to loved ones about this and that.
While he's ashore he'll drink a few beers,
  A vodka and splash will help on the cheers.

Not until Sunday did we finish load.
  Then on the tide it's back down the road.
Outwards to Rotterdam with this load of scarp.
  Well clear of the Toung; the mate a mishap.
In previous days he'd complained of his back.
  Mounting his seat he'd not used the knack.

A 'medico' call through North Foreland was made.
  Dover coastguard said plans had been laid
Back towards Ramsgate for a 'medivac'.
  When it's completed cap's back to his sack.
For not till the morning could a new mate join us.
  Sailing on Sunday no more of a fuss.
Arriving on Monday at two of the clock.
  Making fast in that Rotterdam dock.

A survey conducted by seven-thirty,
  Discharge completed well after tea.
Sailing for Vlaadingen to load up with rods.
  Out of flavour with chartering gods.
For this cargo's destined a bit of a freak.
  We're loading for 'Pinns', on Barking Creek.

Nevil

Finch (continues)

Sixth of June departure from Vlaadingen this day,
    Silken smooth seas around us as we speed on our way.
But time will wait for no man; we're late at Sea Reach One,
    Twenty minutes behind hand; for sure the tide has gone.
Past Gravesend we pushed her up to the Dartford Bridge,
    There is no chance on this tide for filling up the fridge.
So back to Gravesend and anchor awaiting the next high tide,
    Sleep is out of the question; that bloody heat inside.

The afternoon sun is burning as we're anchor up and aweigh,
    Bound for the wharfs at Barking to sit on the stinking clay.
There on Friday morning the discharge was commenced,
    Our new radar's fitted, the captain's well recompensed.
Saturday's omnibus of 'Brookside' I watched in the sweltering mess,
    Slipping the wharfs of Barking and cleared the silted Ness.
Berthed head up at Erith the vegetable oilseed works,
    Loaders work all hours; it really gives the jerks.

But heavy rain descending put stop to plans on load,
    It is not long after that we are up the road.
The loading is completed by noon time next day,
    Alas the ship is grounded. So there we had to stay.
All free crew now muster and down the road they stride,
    Returning individually to sail on the evening tide.
Patiently we waited, on the first of ebb we sail,
    Out through the Princess channel no problem we entailed.

South bound through the Goodwins passing Dover it's quite clear,
    Into the south-west traffic lanes to the Greenwich Buoy did steer.
Cape Hage is our next way point, across the north-east lane.
    Our new radar's terrific; it's not the usual pain.
The course line lies south-westerly through the Alderney race,
    The tide is in our favour, Oh! what a cracking pace.
Past the island of Guernsey, between Jersey and Sark,
    When we come off Tregier, my goodness what a lark.

No pilot out to meet us; their fees have not been paid,
    We have to drop our anchor and there we should have stayed.
Now at the very last moment the order comes through,
Berthed, this Breton harbour with the agent all-a-stew.
    He is faxing and is phoning to straighten up the mess,
I'm straight to a quayside cafe taking out the stress.
    The sun blazed down remorseless from a cloudless sky,
Far too hot for me, though I think that I will fry.

In evening cool I wander and to a chateau go,
Madam Beachie the owner a tremendous character, you know.
Her wine cellar she's refurbished into a seaman's club,
To mariners in this port this is their social hub.
This lady's over seventy a good friend she makes of most,
Sailors worldwide know her as the Mama host.

Thursday's sun remorseless completed late that morn,
Sailing for Parr that evening to be there by the dawn.
This Cornish port is noted for ice coat all year round,
China clay dust abundant covers all above ground
Loading completed in sunshine by mid afternoon,
Lucky that I see friends that are retiring soon.
Cyril and Mavis Jenkins, hosts of the famous Parr Inn,
Retire from a lifetime serving, they say it with a grin.

Now there's a last minute panic before we can set sail,
A blundered bunker delivery, how could the office fail?
So now we are diverted to magnificent Plymouth Sound,
Bunkered from *Onward Mariner*, this barge is much renowned.
Then up the channel we're plodding into an easterly chop,
The television reception is not a lot of cop.
For Saturday is exciting it is the big, big match,
The Scottish efforts thwarted by a brilliant catch.

Sunday dawn saw Dover, by breakfast well out of sight,
North-easterly we are heading into the German Bight.
Monday we are passing the fair Friesian Isles,
Then later in the evening piloting Wesser miles.
Tuesday morning in Bremen, passing Obleshousen locks,
Oh! how I am hoping reload's inside these docks.
I sit now in my cabin awaiting the agent's news,
Do we load in this port, or is it the ballast blues?

Nevil

Finch (still continues)

Last Wednesday morn from Bremen we sail,
    Into the Bight and a north-west gale.
West through the inshore traffic zone,
    The damned bloody rolling aches every bone.
Heading south by Thursday's dawn,
    No sleep for crew we're quite forlorn.
Ymuiden's distinct if the horizon is clear,
    Great plumes of smoke pollution I fear.
In through the piers by ten o' clock,
    Port side secured in the outer dock.
Giant cranes load the cargo pre-slung,
    In hours few our journey's begun.
Bundles of re-rods for Port Coueron,
    I've never berthed there but passed it and on.
This desolate quay on the banks of the Loire,
    To pilot this river's cap's French favourite by far.
Midnight North Hinder by one mile we pass,
    Then down to Ramsgate for cooking gas.
South-west down channel to Sandown Bay,
    Once again to anchor we lay.
Not one of the crew understood this move,
    A six hour stay and cap would prove.
This crafty old salt is working the tide,
    It will pay handsome on the French side.
The channel Le Fours only open by day,
    If you lose out it's a hell of a way.
Out to the Atlantic, well clear of the isles,
    If you can time it saves sixty odd miles.
Sunday a dodder in flat calm seas,
    Strong is the sun; not even a breeze.
Heading south-east passed Bell Isle inside,
    We'll have to anchor or push the ebb tide.
Anchor that night, under way by six,
    Passing the buoys as the morning sun licks.
Berthing by ten the agent's Allier,
    Short notice given, no dockers are there.
Discharge commenced in afternoon sun,
    Down to the town for a spot of fun.
A local young lady with broken motorbike,
    Crew mend it for favours, alas she's a dyke.

Tuesday's a smelter; I'm eaten alive,
    Even at midnight my cabin's sixty-five.
Cool is the morn as the cargo's complete,
    Noon temperature's rising I feel quite deplete.
Sailing for Par as slight are the seas,
    God, how I hope for a cooling breeze
Now we are traversing our reverse track,
    Wishing that this place I'm not back.
Thursday's dawn brings overcast sky,
    At least this day I shall not fry.
Ushant Isle lies eastward ten miles,
    England's defeat brings no crew smiles.
Arriving too late at Tywadreath Bay,
    This night at anchor we had to stay.
At four in the morning the pilot on board,
    Two hours later the first lorry is poured.
The cargo came slowly brought from the sticks,
    To get the night in we'd need a few tricks.
Try as they might for the evening tide,
    We are determined to be alongside.
High water passed as the last load is tipped,
    Slow as a snail the hatch lids are flipped.
Slowly the sailors work top dogs and side,
    No chance now of sailing this tide.
So down to the mission and out on the town,
    Not like the eighties; the place was renown.
A hen party gathered in the Parr Inn late,
    The poor girl deliberates what is her fate.
So back to the ship with a sway in our walk,
    Back in the mess we supper and talk.
Then off to bed for a few hours' kip,
    At four in the morning I'm on my last trip.
Outwards to Dordrecht and back to where?
    Hoping for calm seas and weather fair.
For next UK port I'm on my rest,
    Back home to Islay to be with the best.

Nevil

Finch (concludes)

From Dordrecht through to Ghent,
By inland waterway.
Via Volkrack, Kramer and Hansweart,
It is a long, long way.
South down the Schelt to Ternuzen,
Into the mighty West Lock.
Onwards past three bridges,
To the steelworks dock.
Hatches open, closed and opened,
Then closed again for night.
We have all been up for so long,
All of us could bite.
Now in the morning open,
For the cargo to complete.
Once again we're sailing,
Just a little deplete.
A choppy passage forecast,
South-westerly five or six.
We hug the Belgian coastline,
As the distance meter clicks.
The F3 buoy's the middle,
It's the busiest I have seen.
All the ships are plotted,
On our new radar screen.
Now abeam North Foreland,
Calling London port control.
They send us to the anchorage,
I'm sure they have no soul.
At midday on Thursday,
We're anchor up and away.
By Sea Reach One we're boarded,
Cap don't mind a pilot today.
For when he gets to Millwall,
His relief waits on the quay.
Then on his way to Islay,
One month he should be free.

Nevil

The Humber pilot service

The River Humber is wrongly described.
It is an *estuary*, both shallow and wide.
Born at the spill of the Trent and the Ouse.
Twisting and turning it's not for abuse.
The Vikings used it; they did not balk,
The Romans used it to fortify York.
Now in the hands of a Conservancy Board,
Ships ply up and down with great safety accord.
Most have a pilot to advise the master,
Some go without their skills no vaster.
For an accent Hull school called Trinity House,
Established to train boys no captain to grouse.

In years gone by, a cutter was on station,
By lamp and flag take ships on rotation.
From cutter to ship by small boarding boat,
The pilot transferred after being afloat.
There are still a few places pilots board this way,
All are abroad none in the UK.
In the mid seventies a boarding update,
Using a fast launch the cadets thought great.
Building a control tower at the tip of Spurn,
Erosion though gives mounting concern.
To speed out a pilot as ships approach,
Or guide them to anchor without reproach.

Back in the eighties there were districts then.
Gooley's, Trenty's and lower station men.
Spurn Point to Vicy Pier he'd then disembark.
Rounding up of Albert Dock seems always in the dark.
A Goole man or a Trenty, dependent where bound,
These men do the steering; they're really quite sound.
The Trent men quite generous with a lift through to Hull,
So long as it's not spring tides when their bus was full.
From Goole it was more difficult they'd be away damned quick,
To catch this fellow's generosity you had to be 'rite slick'.
A further complication as Goole splits into two,
A Hull man inwards; out a Goolie to do.

Timing is most critical for an upper river berth,
Low water revealing the shifting mounds of earth.
When tide is low you cannot go with anything that's large,
There really is not enough to sail a ballast barge.
A narrow slot on every tide when numerous pilots muster,
At a prime called 'Boarding Time', when ships set off in a cluster.
It's four and a half hours before next high water Hull,
From designated anchorages at the Hawk or Bull.

Now the service rationalised for great efficiency,
Pilots take you all the way without deficiency.
You're boarded at anchor or passing the Spurn Float,
He's despatched from the landing stage in a high speed boat.
From Hull he may have driven in one of many cars,
Two hours notice given; surely their wives are stars.

Now a mythical passage on a ship from overseas,
We've loaded steel in Bremen bound for Wharton's Quays.
Our passage nearly over, Humber light ship shows on screen.
Spurn pilot we are calling on VHF, fourteen.
'Spurn pilot, Spurn pilot this is the *Lochindaal*'.
'*Lochindaal Lochindaal* Spurn Pilots, receiving your call'.
'Spurn pilot the *Lochindaal* I've a four metre draft,
Our ETA ten-thirty, and the ladder's port side aft'.
'Lochindaal Spurn pilot, thanks for that,
You've a ready berth so keep the handles flat.
Five miles from the Light Float give another shout,
The pilot will board you a couple of miles out'.
Past the Spurn light float to Checker buoys next,
Shape up to the point end not becoming perplexed
Iris speeds towards us showing a white over red.
(The student's aid to remember is a girl in your bed.)
The launch gently touches after sweeping around our stern,
Our pilot jumps aboard us, he's showing great concern.
He knows we are not speedy, and we're a little late,
If we do not berth on this tide it's another date.
As the tides are falling, that's going from spring to neap,
Should we stick on this tide the owner will have a weep.
We have to be most vigilant keeping her on track,
For if there is a grounding, for sure there will be flak.

Pass south of the Hawk light float making two-nine-two,
The leading lights at Killingholm, they will keep us true.
Report to VTS Humber as we pass buoy sixty-three,
Thank God that we're not stopping at Riverside quay.
Shaping up for Salt End through the Foul Holm channel.
I banter with the pilot, he's not taking any flannel,

Now abeam the Paul Sands buoy reporting once more.
Vigilantly watching should she start to yaw.
Safe into the south channel at the Elbow buoy,
Pushing her, pushing her, full power we deploy.
We'll soon be passing under the longest suspension bridge,
Give full attention steering or we'll ground upon a ridge.

Report again to VTS once under this huge structure.
The engine cooling system, is coming close to a rupture.
Once past Brough we've time enough the throttles we can ease,
Just in time as thermos climb, that's made me really pleased.
'Tween Whittons and the Walker Dykes the tide begins to slow,
Report once more to VTS we now don't say, 'Cheerio'.

Now this approach to Apex is the place that we most fear,
For it is on the exact that we will have to steer.
The tide rip is atrocious as it splits into two,
If we're out of position the ship will surely slew.
Round the bend safely, and on the leading light,
This manoeuvre over our nerves are not so tight.

Under the wires at Garthorpe on past Kings Ferry wharf,
The giant cranes at Flixborough, our ship dwarf.
Now we're clear of Neaphouse where we can start our swing,
Rounding up head to tide full power before berthing.
Grove Berni and Mick are boatmen they will take our ropes,
They think of masters and pilots as the most useless dopes.

Now we're secured and my seamanship's done,
I might be thinking of a spot of fun.
The pilot, alas, his work's not complete,
He's to drive back to Hull after a colleague to meet.
For not till he's back to the centre of town,
Can he drive home and get his head down.

Calum McK

The captain's missing chicken leg

Oh! Crew of the *Laurel*, please listen to me,
That leg of a chicken, I held back from my tea.
When I got back, from a stroll on the shore.
It's not on the plate, as it was before.
All information, in strict confidence
From this thieving fellow I'll need recompense.

M. McKenzie Crum

The slick bicki nicker

There is a bicki nicker,
Upon this Lapthorne ship.
He's slick this bicki nicker,
As in the tin he'll dip.
If this slick bicki nicker,
Knows what's good for him,
The slick bicki nicker,
Will keep his hand, *out* the tin.

M. McKenzie Crum

The Lochindaal Hotel

I have been that wild rover for twenty odd years,
I've drunk lots of whisky, and most of the beers.
I've traded from Ventspile down to the Med,
From the Shannon to Karlsrhue I've nursed a sore head.

I sailed from Landskrona bound to Runcorn,
When we put into Islay when our bow became torn
'Twas the Islay lifeboat that answered our call,
In the Lochindaal Bar they welcomed us all.

Ian's the owner; he's known for his smile,
Derick's his barman; he'll serve you with style.
Linda the barmaid will give you her mind,
If you're being impatient or a tiresome bind.

Big Alister Maclellan sits at the bar,
Bertie Anderson stands, but not very far.
Archie Maclellan pops in for his nips,
With Donnie Monro, he's worked on the ships.

Ted Sykes is a regular among farmers galore,
Ivor Drinkwater, the painter, and many a more.
There's Donnie Clark and Donnie the post,
I've even heard talk of a real friendly ghost.

Pauline's one regular who comes from afar
Her dress code sensations make her the star.
Margeret's another who visits a friend.
Whilst visitors returning is much of a trend.

On Saturday nights a ceilidh band plays,
Alec the moony performs through the haze.
Tunes from his squeeze box are heard in the street,
With Ian Mackinnan; his piping's a treat.

Tony Dance gives a song in magnificent voice,
The 'Floral Dance' his favoured choice.
Many local musicians join in this jam,
Few of the patrons not giving a damn.

Now my wild drinking I've decided to leave,
Till my time back in Islay, you've got to believe.
In the Lochindaal Hotel I'll lift my jar,
There at this timeless Hebridean bar.

Calum Mck

Maas Approach Radar

Mass approach radar scans well out to sea,
At thirty-fives miles they're watching me.
By buoy Mike Whisky one I make myself known,
Even at this range my echo is shown.
On zero one I give my call sign,
Deepest draft, ETA, and safety points fine.
At Mike Whisky three I report once again,
No pilot required so south in the lane.
Eastward our passage through inner traffic scheme,
Every move plotted on large radar screen.
Mike Whisky five, and the channel is changed,
Our radar too is now down range.
Channel zero two for the 'Pilot Maas',
Any mistake and I'll show as an ass.
Altering course for buoy *MV Noord*,
Changing the channel for 'mass entrance' co-ords.
Now zero three and line up the reds,
Into the waterway past ferry boat sheds.
Chop to six five for Rosenborough's say,
Through the vast flood gates they have their way.
Starboard post seven is cleared without fuss,
Change to eight zero for Sector 'Maasluss'.
Then onto Botleck, the busiest bar none,
Working there traffic on channel six one.
On past factories and heavy industry,
'Eemshaven' listen on channel six three.
Passing vast docklands for yachts a 'No go'.
Sector 'Waalhven' covers on channel 'six zero'.
Now sighting Park quay the berth that's right on,
Report to 'Maasbridges' on channel eight one.
All fast and finished prepare for a spree,
Don't forget 'Traffic centre' on channel one three.

Calum Mck

Monarch of the Sea

The crimson sun sank slowly,
　　Behind the deep dark cloud.
　　The August mist around us,
The radar showing proud.
As sky draws ever darker,
　　One blip stands out most clear.
What was this echo showing?
　　As slowly it did near.
I laid off all the vectors.
　　A fisherman I'd supposed.
We'd clear her holding steady.
　　A risk she did not propose.
Binoculars trained to starboard.
　　To confirm this radar blip.
One bright red light is spotted.
　　This was no fishing ship.
Last light of dusk had dwindled.
　　Just enough to see.
Tall masts with billowed canvas.
　　A monarch of the sea.

Four huge masts stand skywards.
　　With acres of canvas set.
White the hull is painted.
　　And polished brass I bet.
This stately lady's progress.
　　Powered only by the breeze.
To cross the head of this one.
　　Would be an act of sleaze.
So hard to starboard we alter.
　　To pass this bright red light
Then round her stern in reverence.
　　As she passed into the night.
Now back on course for England.
　　Two engines raging tone.
How my heart is with that tall ship.
　　Whose aura is her own.

Calum Mck

Dolphin

From the moment that telephone rang for me,
Oh! what a drag to go back to sea.
An overnight drive to the office at Hoo,
To sail a ship; not return to you.

From Tower wharf on the Thames,
Duty on this should make amends.
Sailing to Calais and shuttle to Kent,
Whitstable the port that we'll be sent.

Supposedly five loads with chance of more,
Receivers can't take so we stop at four.
Now we're bound for Rotterdam port,
Highplat's the village; the stay will be short.

Steel is the cargo then bound north-west,
Into the Humber I expect some guests.
Brad for the Becks then Angie with kids,
In no time at all we're closing the lids.

From New Holland dock we ballast our ways,
Ymiden the port; we lay there three days.
The billet's not ready the factory must make,
Sailed to Kings Lynn without our full take.

Berthing there Thursday in early eve.
Goodbyes on Friday, but I'm not on leave.
Not a long journey, though four trains I must ride,
Goole is the harbour, the *Swan* cap shall guide.

Nevil

Swan

We lay at Goole the weekend,
Most family I saw.
Summer sun abundant,
I could not have asked for more.
Discharging on the Monday,
Then sailing after tea.
Ballasting to Vlaardingen,
On a flat calm sea.
Load delays on Wednesday,
As heavy rain foils.
Brought by barge from Hungary,
These sixty-three coils.
Our cargo now secured,
Cap's last mail's been sent.
This loads destination,
Is Newport, Gwent.
Out through the Hook of Holland,
To follow the traffic scheme.
South-westerly past Dover,
As countless ships are seen.
Westwards now to Land's End,
Oh! what a glorious day,
High clouds start to thicken,
In moments it is grey.
For sure a cold front's passing,
Squally seas soon buffet the bow.
Loose items stowed securely,
As we are rolling now.
The coastguards at Falmouth,
By radio they're advised.
That through the inshore traffic zone,
Our sail plan is revised.
Once round the Longship lighthouse,
The seas are from astern.
The rolling it is easing,
And so is our concern.
North-east and then to eastward,
To the Breaksea buoy.

Told we must drop anchor,
Much to skip's annoy.
For as no ships are sailing,
From out of Newport docks.
No personnel are rostered,
To operate the locks.
In Cardiff Roads we're lying,
For over twenty hours.
Berthing Newport Sunday,
As heavy rain showers.
Monday no discharging,
It's August bank holiday.
Tuesday we are finished,
To speed upon our way.
A sail plan set to Ireland,
The small port of Arklow.
Fertiliser is the cargo,
To Moordyke we shall go.
Sailing on the Thursday,
Before the chimes of noon.
We may well see Cornwall,
By the end of the moon.
By ten o' clock next morning,
Land's End has passed abeam.
High pressure holds above us,
Good passage is foreseen.
South of Rundelstone marker,
Cleared Lizard point safe.
Steering for the Greenwich light buoy,
We're no ocean waif.
Saturday's dawn is overcast,
With slightly rippled sea.
Passing the Greenwich light buoy,
As I sit down for tea.
Sunday turns exciting,
A most pleasurable day.
Into the Schelt via the 'Rhumpot',
I've never been this way.

Berthed at the desolate Moordyke,
By eight that summer's eve,
Too far from the city,
A shore run we shall leave.
Monday's prompt discharging,
Came to an abrupt halt.
The cargo is rejected,
Thank God, it's not our fault.
We're shifted to a lay-by,
For experts to review.
A lift with the agent to Dordrecht,
For now I can scuttle a few.
Tuesday we're back to discharge,
As quality experts arrive,
How I hope they'll finish,
So we vacate this dive.
Alas, our hopeful departure,
Is not to be this day.

The sifter it's not working,
So here we have to stay.
I take a walk in the evening,
To the nearest bar.
All closed when I arrive there,
So back it is from far.
Wednesday the hatches opened,
For work to start on time.
The prospects constantly changing,
But we are finished fine.
Just a few moments later,
We're back upon our way.
Ballasting to Limehouse,
A wharf on the River Medway.

Nevil

Swan (continues)

From Thursday into Friday,
　　At Limehouse wharf we lay.
Making fast at Queenborough,
　　Late that sunny day.

On Saturday morn they started,
　　The cargo coming slow.
Not till late on Monday,
　　We slip our ropes and go.

We wend our way to the Medway,
　　Pilot and trainee on board.
Safe past the sunken *Montgomery*,
　　and out towards the Nord.

Via the Princess to Margate,
　　Then Gull Stream to the Straight.
South-westerly through the Channel,
　　How this trip shows my hates.

Tuesday is a dull day,
　　Slight seas from abaft the beam.
By midnight the Channel light buoy,
　　As countless ships are seen.

Wednesday's dull and overcast,
　　As slight the seas remain.
In evening rounding Ushant,
　　To cross the Bay again.

Thursday's dawn was crimson,
　　With puffs of cumulus cloud.
Slight now the ship is rolling,
　　As round us dolphins crowd.

Thick cloud to the east on Friday,
　　The sun was late to shine.
Endless ships stream past us,
　　Off 'Cabo Villano' we shall dine.

A hazy sunrise Saturday,
　　From a clear Portuguese sky.
In afternoon our arrival,
　　Surely we shall fry.

Sunday's sun outstanding,
　　As boat drill we complete.
Jollied to the beach at Barrie;
　　That really was a treat.

Monday's discharge completed,
　　In warm torrential rain.
To Lexioes and to an anchor,
　　Oh! what a goddamned pain.

For thirteen hours we're waiting,
　　For the next daytime tide.
How we all are wishing,
　　They'd let us lie inside.

Tuesday's passage to Sardura,
　　Beautiful beyond belief.
Skimming bridges by centimetres,
　　Berthing with light relief.

Nevil

Swan (Portugal - The Baltic)

We loaded granite in Sardura,
But that's another tale.
Out to sea on Friday,
Into a north-west gale.
Friday night we're rolling,
Tossed from side to side.
Into a Spanish valley,
We'll surely go and hide.
But no we keep on steaming,
North-west to the traffic scheme.
The weather forecast promising,
So we push on it seems.
Saturday is unforgiving,
As gale drops down to breeze.
Yet still the endless rolling,
From those relentless seas.
Sunday's seas decreasing,
Under a dull overcast sky.
To say this trip I'm enjoying,
would be an outright lie.

By Monday nearing Ushant,
Captain's link call to the shore
My relief's been re-directed,
Oh! what a blinking bore.
Late afternoon round Ushant,
North-east to the CLV
Watching for 'cellphone' reception,
And hoping for British TV.
Tuesday's calm conditions,
But no TV today.
On deck the crew are working,
Tom confirms my continuing stay.
Wednesday's dawn at the Sandette,
At the Texal by near midnight.
Two thirds the passage over,
Some food is getting tight.
Thursday's dawn sky threatens,
dark and overcast.
South-east gales are imminent,
From the BBC's forecast.

Heavy cloud above us,
    Shroud the eclipse of the moon.
Passing into the Skagerrak,
    By late Friday afternoon.
Rough seas set upon us,
    As we clear Skagen Noord.
Sheltered after midnight,
    In a Swedish fjord.
Berthing at Stenungsund,
    By four that Saturday morn.
Fresh bright daylight revealing,
    What a joy to be born.
Idyllic chocolate box houses,
    With private jetty and berths.
The Swedes are much admired,
    For acquiring all these worths.
The discharge gang commencing,
    By half past eight o' clock.
Not till afternoon Sunday,
    Had they got their pile of rock.
Off upon completion,
    By last light of the day.

What a breathtaking passage,
    Magnificent all the way.
Clearing the Marstrund Fyjorden,
    Heading to the south and west.
Crossing the busy Katagat,
    The speed is at our best.
Self pilot into Randers,
    It took a lot of skill.
Safely the ship secured,
    For sure gave all a thrill.
Final discharge commencing,
    Soon after we arrive.
How the Rinns I'm missing,
    How shall I ever survive?
The discharge finally completed,
    On Tuesday afternoon.
Sailing directly for Bergstaaken.
    To be there just as soon.

Nevil

Swan (concludes)

They sent us to Burgstraaken,
     A German island port.
The people were quite friendly,
     Most were the tourist sort.

The loading started Wednesday.
     Pouring wheat into the night.
In the *Kniper* we gathered,
     To put the world to rights.

At half past six on Thursday,
     Clearance papers came on board.
This day a special holiday,
     Six years of unified co-ord.

By seven o clock we're outbound,
     The water's dropping fast.
Scraping through the channel,
     to deeper water at last.

Only three courses this passage,
     Two hundred miles to go.
To a tiny Polish harbour,
     A resort called Darlowo.

The daytime is terrific,
     Light seas and brilliant sun.
Maybe at Darlowo,
     The lads will find some fun.

Through the narrow entrance,
     At first of Friday's light.
My old ship is working,
     Breydon Venture such a sight.

Both crews are keen to gossip,
     Pop up the town to shop.
And on the Friday evening,
     They find a local hop.

Discharging starts on arrival,
     Continues day and night.
Not until Sunday morning,
     The last grains are out of sight.

In shifts we took our free time,
     For social integrate.
The disco 'Magic Jumpers';
     A hot spot for my mates.

At eight-fifteen on Sunday,
     Officials board our ship.
All bureaucracy completed,
     Our mooring ropes we slip.

We're ballasting to Bremen,
     To load at Klockner Staal.
Coils and other products,
     But not for the River Waal.

This lot's for Bilbao,
     The canal Ducto no doubt.
But I'm not doing this one.
     It's the permanent master's shout.

Nevil

Visiting the Tyne

When I was a lad I'd visit the Tyne,
To my uncle's house on the electric line.
By double-deck bus I'd come from Hull,
Not even a radio but it wouldn't be dull.
Our comics and mags would be saved for a while,
They'd be beside us in a great pile.
On bumpy old roads that weren't very grand,
Before rebuilding this war-torn land.

Through Beverley, Weighton, Pocklington and York.
Then Easingwold, Thirsk and Northallerton fork.
After we stopped for a tinkle and tea,
Journeyed through Spennymoor and Pity Me.
The Great North Road magnificently named,
Three tracks wide, and poorly maintained.
This East Yorkshire bus had accomplished some feat,
As we sped through the hills round Chester-le-Street.

Passed Gateshead town and over the Tyne,
Into the Haymarket the journey's been fine.
Though an unheard plea from a lad in short pants,
Rough moquette seats had bit deeper than ants.
Uncle would meet us; he'd be in his car,
Out to Monkseaton, that's not very far.
To stay up here a week or ten days,
We'd soon be into the Geordie ways.

With Pamela, my cousin, we're acting as one,
The cause of some trouble then we'd be gone.
Jumping the train to Whitley Bay,
At Spanish City the machines we'd play.
This seaside mecca gave great delight,
How we wished we could do it at night.
If we had time we'd ride the full loop,
If asked for our tickets she'd just cock a snoop.

This was exciting as you ran by the Tyne,
The industrial giants, were not in decline.
Seemed every foot of this great river's banks,
Had thriving shipyards and factories for tanks.
My Uncle was Staff Officer RNVR *Tyne*,
When we went for a picnic that boat would be mine.
I'd vie with my brother to steer through Tyne bridge,
I must have been a bossy young tidge.

In a twenty-two foot open motor boat,
With me at the helm it's the finest afloat.
I would stand on the thwart quite sublime,
This was the finest ship of the line.
I'd strut the boat proud the first lord of the sea,
Back down that night I'd be curled on dad's knee.
Then when the time came to go back to Hull,
My heart was on Tyneside Oh! what a pull.

When I was a likely lad, I'd visit the Tyne,
I'd come in the car of a pal of mine.
He was a rep for plastic bags,
You just wouldn't believe some of the gags.
The road now dual with some motorway,
We could speed North not taking all day.
Making his calls on the way up,
We'd stop for our lunch and something to sup.

A few more calls after our break,
Then a hotel we knew on the make.
Shower and shave, we'd make ourselves slick,
Down to the town pretty damn quick.
The club Dolci Vita suited us fine,
That seemed the focus for girls round the Tyne.
How we would pull, or thought we could,
Till the girls from Felling told us were dud.

Every year he'd change his car,
Mind you though it had been wide and far.
From the Ford retailer in Whitley Bay,
His choice of colour was always gay.
'It's no use', he said 'changing your wheels,
If the neighbours don't notice I'm doing the deals.'
But a custard yellow Cortina estate,
Was not the best for the girls to relate.

When doing this deal we'd stay at the Bay,
The Sands Hotel was the place to play.
Many a rep' from near and far,
Had come to drink that Geordie jar.
The girls were there in all their splendour,
From grossly fat to ever so slender.
We made our play telling small lies,
The girls too smart for us Yorkie guys.

Now we're older cross the Tyne we speed,
Uncle's a boat at Berwick on Tweed.
He'll give me a loan to enjoy the sport,
Just so long as we make port to port.
At the Harrow at Tweedmouth we'd plan our voyage,
Like Vikings of past to plunder and forage.
First to Eyemouth then Lindisfarne.
Into the inns we'd drink and yarn.

There is no denying as we made our way south,
To Amble, Blyth, and in at Tynemouth.
When we ran up the Tyne be it such a boat,
I know straight away there's a lump in my throat.
The memories flood back as Wallsend we pass,
The times that I'd had with a Geordie lass.
Now on the reach that the bridge comes to sight,
To be back on the Tyne, Oh! what a delight!

Calum Mck

Sardura stevedores

Tuesday's berthing at Sardura,
    Was late in the afternoon.
Hoards of people board us,
    They load till the light of moon.

Agents, stevedores and officials,
    Call for a loading plan.
By sunset of that evening,
    That plan well down the pan.

They loaded kerbs a thwart ships,
    Not as the mate had planned.
They slipped some under the cupboards,
    Now that was underhand.

By close of work on Tuesday,
    They said 'All kerbs are on.
Start eight o' clock on Wednesday,
    Loading blocks to separation.'

Only our crew had noticed,
    A lorry load of kerb.
How this late delivery,
    would jar the shippers nerve.

Loaded two hours later,
    Atop a separation wall.
The captain called for securing,
    For they would surely fall.

The agent said, 'You're joking,
    we don't do that sort of thing.'
The captain said they had to,
    'Or the ship will stay till spring.'

They chocked these kerbs with Big Bags,
    Filled with granite blocks.
If this was good securing,
    I'd eat my blinking socks.

Thursday's sailing was cancelled,
    For experts to attend.
They studied it profusely,
    And banded in the end.

Just what the captain had asked for,
    From Wednesday afternoon.
If only they had acted,
    The ship would have sailed so soon.

Friday's dawn departure,
    Down the river Doura.
Let's hope that next time they listen,
    And maka the cargo secura.

Calum McK

Golf's hallowed ground

Though I've been a sailor most of my life,
For golfers their mecca's the Kingdom of Fife.
From there on the TV I've seen the great crowd,
Supporting their heroes, and cheering so loud.
My ship was secured at a quay on the Tay,
I'd visit the centre of serious play.
I walked the main street of this 'Varsity town,
Then through a side cut I turned down.

From the sea front a sight beyond true,
As the Royal and Ancient came into view.
I strolled the prom approaching this seat,
Then for some tea, and to rest up my feet.
The cafe itself a place of renown,
As I take up a table, staff give a frown.
They thought they'd finished yet had to serve me,
My buttered scone is plonked down without glee.

Half consumed when the bucket arrived,
To mop round our feet in a manor contrived.
I was determined to keep my seat,
So stared out the window, not being defeat.
Oh what a vista; the whole course is seen,
The red flag fluttered over a perfect green.
The eighteenth hole what gratification;
To hark and hole is pure exhilaration.

To lead at this while 'The Open' is played,
Was in the dreams of our man portrayed.
While members viewed from resplendent bay,
They could only stand and gaze.
I remember the blazer its colour light blue,
The guy stood in reverence a homage to few.
He's stood on that path the masters have trod,
His shoes not touching one blade of the sod.

He was playing the last as he stood sublime,
The crowds were cheering as he stroked so fine.
He'd birdied and eagled as he played that course,
Brought back to life and utter remorse.

His wife who'd been shopping spotted him there,
She's walking towards him to show off her ware.
His heart missed a beat as she steps on *that* green,
He's making a signal; it's not to be seen.
To 'stop' in her tracks and 'Go back to the street',
Should Bonallack's staff see the marks of her feet.
Alas poor girl she's walked too far,
Another sign and her pride would jar.

Her bags thrown down with dramatic airs,
Glad not to catch those cutting glares.
She stamped her feet and turned on spot,
What was his problem? The silly clot.
Back she stomped by another track,
That perfect green her high heels hack.
As off she strides towards the town,
That guy's heart has sunk right down.

He hardly dares lift his face,
Just followed on in total disgrace.
I don't know how this domestic ends,
Though I bet that night they're not best friends.
Should you take your partner to this hallowed ground,
Keep them to heel, like a well-trained hound.
You'll accomplish your dream, with the winning stroke,
Not follow your partner, you wish to choke.

Calum McK

Failte Calidonian Maca Bhruthainn
(Welcome to Caledonian MacBrayne)

It's in Gaelic you're welcomed, on board this fine ship.
On a sailing to Islay, whatever your trip.
Be it business or pleasure, you'll come the same way.
Through the finest of vistas, your journey will lay.
From Glasgow the road is carved out of rock.
Down past the side of the world's favourite loch;
Loch Lomond of course - its sights are a feast.
Tarbet's the place, travellers join from the east.
Westward to Arrachar and the head of Loch Long.
Climbing Glen Coe your heart fills with song,
'Rest and be Thankful' lies at the top.
Through Glen Kinglas, great views as you drop.
Descending to Cairndow and the banks of Loch Fyne.
Where the most famous kippers, were smoked on a line.
West the road lies, over an ancient stone bridge
Inveraray's the place, to buy fish for the fridge.
Bypassing Furness, on to Lochgilphead.
Aside the banks of Loch Fyne, your problems are shed.
At Ardrishaig, there's the Crinan canal
Searching the loch, for a visiting mammal.

Tarbet's the place, if you're to renege,
Only six miles to Kennacraig.
Big Kenny will greet you, with a boarding pass.
A tape he has ready to check the car's class.
Some Land Rover drivers will argue the point.
Even removing the front bumper's tow joint,
Waiting in queues for embarkation.
Turning and backing to a mates deliberation.
Leave your car, and enter the accommodation.
Some head to the bar, for fortification.

Promenade the decks, though the breeze may be strong.
If you sit in the lounge, you won't go wrong.
For over two hours you'll be under way
That's to Port Ellen or Port Askaig
When the ship is secured, you're off in a crush.
In no time at all, you've forgotten the rush.
Wherever you stay, in the Rinns or the Oa
It's a terrible wrench, when the time comes to go.
Islay's renowned for tranquillity,
Served by MacBrayne's reliability.

Calum McK

Laurel

O h, when we parted at Berwick upon Tweed,
    In different directions we had to speed.
You to the Rinns, the place I adore,
    Me to the south that journey a bore.

By overnight sleeper to Dover in Kent,
    To pick up the *Laurel* I'm hell bent.
She's lying outside stemming the seas,
    Tossed around in more than a breeze.

Finally docking late Thursday night,
    Booked into the mission I'm all right.
Nick is the master, who's going on leave,
    He's got an offer tucked up his sleeve.

Duty starts Thursday discharged at a pace.
    It's the last cargo for this ancient place.
For almost two centuries they've taken stone here,
    The reasons for stopping are not made clear.

So off on the tide to Vamo Mills,
    Soya bean meal our hold will fill.
This factory lies on the outskirts of Ghent,
    To New Holland pier we'll be sent.

Berthing there Sunday ashore to the club,
    Bingo tonight at this social hub.
Striking a deal for a small TV set,
    Vodka was flowing with Danes we met.

Discharge completed by noon on Monday,
    Engineers working so hear we stay.
Their tasks completed by mid afternoon,
    Outwards we're heading pretty damn soon.

Our orders to Rotterdam for an anthracite load,
    It's northerly gales 'I'll be blowed.'
Slamming and rolling of the Norfolk coast,
    Ordered to Park quay we make the most.

The mate goes ashore in his whistle and flute,
    Poking his plastic gets plenty of loot
Down to a dance hall he knows not where,
    Back before sailing his pockets are bare.

At four in the morning we slip this lay-by,
        Beside the *Blue Master* is where we lie.
Called far too early; it's the usual lark,
        The crew up for hours all during the dark.

In daylight they want us; vast floating cranes swing,
        Giant grabs disgorge it's really something.
The loading completed at the back of one,
        Survey completed, and then we are gone.

Out through the piers and into the swell,
        West through the traffic schemes Edd's not well.
Once round North Hinder the seas fall away,
        Now passing Dover he's feeling OK.

Westwards down channel the seas are slight,
        The ships that are passing a magnificent sight.
One of our newest the *Larch* slips past,
        She's bound for Siloth and not all that fast.

A crimson dawn Friday as calm seas remain,
        Rare for these ships some time we shall gain
Now on the radio there's Plymouth pilot,
        No ready berth; is someone a clot?

The *Arklow Valley* is catching us fast,
        She has priority they're working us last.
In radio calls her master suggests
        We lie alongside; he'll make us guests.

In through the east, as he takes the west,
        A pilot will board to take him to rest.
We follow slowly, and swing off the quay.
        Plymouth's the port for a sailor to be.

Nevil

Laurel (Continues)

From Friday through to Sunday,
    Outside the *Valley* we lay.
They accuse us of detention,
    It's they who want to stay.
Discharging on the Monday,
    Departing after tea.
Not a very long passage,
    But gratefully a calm sea.

We washed out on the journey,
    Twenty mile or less.
The hold inspector saw it,
    And considered it a mess.
Descaling and rewashing,
    Took Tuesday's daylight time.
After snipe remarks to the master,
    The inspector said 'It's fine.'

Immediately they're loading,
    As the lads slipped to the Mish.
Helen's with two girlfriends,
    All three are such a dish.
Work stops for night on Tuesday,
    We finish off next day.
Computers go down in the office,
    So there is a short delay.

Chance meeting with a colleague,
    Paul Johnson; we go back.
He's got the *Elizabeth C* now,
    You would not believe the crack.
Eastwards up the Channel,
    The AP's on the blink.
We navigate the old way,
    It makes us have to think.

Friday noon past Flushing,
    We take a pilot today.
A full ebb tide against us,
    He chunters all the way.

The giant locks at Zandfleet,
    Is where we have to go.
Taking a complete lock full,
    They are so blinking slow.
When locking is completed,
    They open the inner gate.
Full speed through the dockland,
    This city stays up late.

Discharging on the Saturday.
    I've never seen such mess.
Grab damage to the steelwork,
    A tank I'll have to press.
We're all cleaned up and shifted,
    Just in time for tea.
It's my first Saturday in Antwerp,
    That I'm not on a spree.

A quiet Sunday morning,
    With visitors afternoon.
My brother and his wife arrive,
    They now live out past Boon.
We talked of family matters,
    Then to a bar for beers.
It's twelve years since I've seen them,
    Let's lift our glass for cheers.

At dusk farewell and departure,
    As we go our separate ways.
They to Antwerp suburbia,
    I to the centre's maze.
A few more drinks then *'Taxi!'*
    To the Mariners Club.
With Mario's warmly welcome.
    It is our Antwerp pub.

A headache Monday morning,
    Long beams they start to load.
Still suffering at lunch time,
    As crew begin to goad.
The dockers now departing,
    Are at the end of shift.
Not till dawn tomorrow,
    Shall we see the final lift.

So with the *Pride* moored by us,
        Once more our crew is out.
I'm hoping in the morning,
        They do not need a shout.
On Tuesday morning, resumption,
        By eight the load's complete.
Gees, we've overloaded,
        We'll have to be discreet.

Compromising with the agent,
        About the loaded weight.
The shipper he's quite adamant,
        there's a hundred tonnes less freight.
Cap's firm about the compromise,
        Thirteen hundred and five.
Twelve thirty-six the shipper says,
        As fax machines come live.

A draft survey is called for,
        At our arrival port.
So eight o' clock on Thursday,
        Cap's patience is quite fraught.
But now the survey's over,
        The captain's been proved right.
More cargo than the compromise,
        It's given him a fright.

Friday's evening departure,
        Bound to the Europort.
North-westerly gales decreasing,
        Is the latest weather report.
Clearing Spurn by midnight,
        Setting the south-easterly course.
By first light we've passed Cromer,
        Those winds have no remorse.

The ship's still pitching and rolling,
        As through the piers we sail.
Hoping when we're outbound,
        These winds will not be gale.

Our destination Europort,
        So line up on the Greens.
Berthing at the coastal pier,
        With many friends it seems.
The agent boarded promptly,
        The paperwork's complete.
Watching videos in the mess room,
        About a Hull fishing fleet.

The video is concluding,
        I'm ready to slip into bed.
A real old friend calls to see me,
        Con Fagen; I thought him dead.
It's coffee that he's drinking,
        And I am on the tea.
Fifteen years or more ago,
        The booze would be running free.

We chatted for over one hour,
        Then he left for his own ship.
He commands the *Union Pluto*,
        Bound Teignmouth this trip.
The time is now past midnight,
        As John is calling home.
You're at the Crofter's ceilidh.
        I listen to generators drone.

In the morning I shall ring you,
        To lighten up my heart.
I know that work is away, dear,
        I can't bear our being apart.

Nevil

Laurel (still continues)

Sullen skies of Sunday morn,
    As we lay at Eurport.
Catching up on paperwork,
    Updating my report.

A walk to the pub at lunch time,
    Two beers and a plate of frits.
This really is a focal point,
    As ten in here are Brits.

Four of the crew from the *Laurel*,
    A welder from the north-east coast.
A lorry driver from Stoke on Trent,
    And the band that's the ferry's toast.

I strolled back to that coastal pier,
    Ships now lay four abreast.
Not a sound from the others though,
    In the past we'd party the rest.

Late Sunday night we're loaded,
    As wind increased to gale.
Decent remarks from the crew are heard,
    They think we should not sail.

In short time out through the piers,
    Into the north-west seas.
Tossed around remorselessly,
    I'd hope that these would ease.

It took nigh twenty-four hours,
    Across to a Norfolk lee.
Then full speed to the Humber,
    A rough one all agree.

No anchoring on Tuesday,
    As straight to the berth we go.
A bout of mechanical failures,
    Was about to give us woe.

First the forward Lister,
    Seas ingress into the exhaust,
Cranking her with vigour,
    To life it couldn't be forced.

Hatch opened by the crane man,
      For grab discharge to commence.
The Cummings split a rubber hose;
      A statement of grievance.

The GS pump was ultimate,
      It would not pump at all.
Forty years experience,
      Was like talking to a wall.

With a positive head of water,
      A Desmi shows the works.
There is no sign of discharge,
      They talk to us like 'Berks'.

Stripping the pipes for access,
      We now can see the cause.
The impeller's off its key way.
      It's got to be 'Sod's law'.

A new pump from the Medway,
      Fitted Thursday afternoon.
Sailing directly for Oldenburg,
      With a port engine plume.

The problem, an air filter,
      Over a year in constant wear.
Now we pass the NAM gas field,
      The weather's turning fair.
A dark dark night of Friday,
      Without a star in the sky.
By dawn the River Wesser,
      At Elsferth we shall lie.

We're just too late to take the tide,
      To Oldenburg this day.
So Sunday morn well after dawn,
      The Hunte's bendy way.

That Saturday night, my God, the crack,
      As three of us drank beers,
A crowd bust in; some dressed to kill,
      Mick thought the lot were queers.

He drank his pint and legged it,
        The quickest I've ever seen.
No way was he enjoying,
        A drink with a drag queen.

This was a joking matter,
        A bit of a pantomime.
Half price drinks for the ladies,
        That's why the guys dressed fine.

These students from the college,
        Putting on the style.
But Elly's overacting,
        He has the sweetest smile.

In freezing fog on Sunday,
        We slipped the ice quay.
A good two hours to Oldenburg,
        We all need lots of tea.

Nevil

Laurel (Christmas approaches)

A Sunday walk to the old town centre,
 A Christmas market just as you enter.
Selling their wares as the temperature froze,
 Crowds of people bright cheeks and red nose.
Then to a bar in a side street,
 Across to the baker for a custard treat.
Reaching the ship I welcomed the warm,
 Back out that night no one's on form.
The local's deserted; so bitter that's why.
 Even the girls appear to be shy.

Six Monday morn grabbing to wharf,
 Afternoon completion we sail to Elsforth.
It's most unusual to stay outbound,
 This is the one time we hang around.
Down in the Keller bar there's Friday night's friend,
 A group of guys on a birthday bend.
Elly's a boy, you can see that for sure.
 I cast my eye on a girl most demure.

Not until Thursday at Kali Kai Bremen,
 Shall we load salt for the Neaphouse weighmen.
In through the locks on Tuesday noon,
 The lads take a walk, but are back pretty soon.
I take a walk but nothing more,
 To look for a cap like I had before.
Back to the ship without success,
 Then watching videos, at ease in the mess.

Wednesday morn as the lads roll the black,
 A lift with a man to the tramway track.
Into the city for a department store,
 I find a cap on the first floor.
Back to the ship for the evening meal,
 Returning with Mick the atmosphere real.
We walked the streets of his vibrant centre,
 Sampled mulled wine and festivities enter.

A beer in two pubs then sausage and chips,
    Boarded a tram to the haunts near the ships.
Finding a bar with plenty of crack,
    Shooting off rockets with a pyromaniac.
With a bundle of these all given free.
    Taxied to ship and a good night for me.

At six Thursday morn the cargo we load,
    By mid afternoon we're well on the road.
Out of the Wesser by ten that night,
    The swell's unreal in the German Bight.
Straight up the Humber no hanging around,
    To Riverside quay and pilot sound.

Onwards up river, dark is the night,
    Rounding for Neaphouse quite a fright.
The main fuel filters have become clogged,
    No power for manoeuvres as engines slogged.
A quick response from Dave, the mate,
    To open the by-pass and save her fate.
Berthing at Neaphouse is a bundle of trouble,
    The shore ropes are sent all a befuddle.

All secured by ten that night,
    Taxi to 'The Jolly' for a pint just right.
We got there the place in full swing,
    Alas, the singer is no king.
Talking to Diane and Cathy too,
    They know the status of Lapthorne crew.
Returning to ship well after time,
    We've had a good laugh; these girls are a dime.

Now it is Sunday I have a free day,
    Lunch with some grandchildren, a pleasure I'll say.
Then in the evening a visitor from Hull,
    Surely my life could never be dull.
Monday at six discharge to the shore,
    The for'd generator's getting a bore.
Once again not showing a thing,
    Down come the fitters for rectifying.

An evening meal with good company,
Back on the ship I rest for a wee.
At twenty-one thirty a pilot on board,
Sailing to Boston where malt will be poured.
Dropping the pilot at Riverside quay,
In patchy fog to the open sea.
When passing the Bull the mate is roused,
Six hours below, yet he still feels drowsed.

Now eight Tuesday morn at anchor we lay,
Hoping the fog will blow away.
Waiting for Boston to give us a call,
When the pilot boat nears the anchor we'll hail.
Inward bound on the morning tide,
The fog so thick there's no riverside.
Slow and safe our passage today,
Berthed at the silo in the sun's weak ray.

Open the hatch but she's still wet,
The silo manager gets into a fret.
He's telexed the office about our conduct,
Into an argument I am sucked.
Being accused of not doing our best,
Condensation the reason she's failing the test.
A hatch left open to capture the breeze,
This inspector we cannot please.

Into the town for a few bits and bobs,
Called in the 'Park' these girls no snobs.
Back on board I'm having a nap,
Tom, the electrician, I almost zap.
The forward generator won't take a load,
A replacement unit he wants on the road.
He's woken me to telephone Hoo,
Surely this is what he could do.

He tightens the connectors; it's on the board,
We think this the answer, so I applaud,
Three hours later it's off again,
God, how this is getting a pain.
I look at the installation and cut out a switch,
It's back on the board; was this the hitch?
At five in the morning the power's not on,
Once again the generator's gone.

Tuesday night's banter with the girls,
Then into the bar Dave he whirls.
In and out as the girls shriek with laughter,
Tomorrow he's leaving, what is he after?
Wednesday morn there's Dennis from Hoo,
Conducting an audit Iso nine thousand and two.
The replacement alternator brought by car,
Tom changes the controller; OK so far.

They started the loading at ten today,
Now past five and their pipe is away.
I've just settled down for Coro' Street,
That generator fails I'll not be beat.
So once again late after tea,
I'm mending the genie but this time glee.
I notice a wire that's chaffed its cover,
Intermittent earth and nothing other.

Wrapping the cable with sticky tape,
The other repairers have they been ape?
Afternoon Thursday Tim Collum arrives,
Once again I'm sensing good vibes.
No cargo loaded due to the rain,
Four a.m. Friday; stand by for grain.

Past ten in the morning, cargo's complete,
The lads can now rest; they're a little deplete.
All is now set to sail on the tide,
We wonder if Christmas we'll be over this side.

Nevil

Laurel (Festive Time)

Off to Rotterdam on the evening tide,
Clear of the Wash rolled side to side.
The north-easterly wind is near to gale,
Most of us look a little pale.
Through the piers early Sunday morn,
In the depth of Siberia this wind was born.
In the bitterest of cold we prepare the hatch,
Swaddled in clothes to leave no bare patch.

No walk at lunch time except to the gate,
By taxi today for our unusual plate.
The normal lunch at the Swiss Chalet Inn,
This time it's me that commits the sin.
Drinking Jennivers as if no tomorrow,
Most certainly drowning all my sorrows.
Back to the ship in time to shift,
Job completed it had been a gift.

At seven on Monday we're on the move,
Slipping the lay-by to discharge approve.
Up and down seeking our place,
Just like being in 'Whacky Race'.
As daylight breaks we find our sucker,
A handrail bent, what a gutter!
A mid-morning delivery of bonded store,
Brought by the girl all adore.

To get these goods from shore to ship,
The 'Kripton Factor' has easier clip.
All hands help in this fatigue,
Soon complete we work as a league.
Now the discharge almost complete,
Our next employment we have to bleat.
Off to Antwerp for an IMCO code,
It's after the holiday this cargo's to load.

Cap's phoning the agent for a lay-by berth,
      For sure that BASF is the end of the earth.
Then a reprieve as we'll load on arrival,
      The inland waterway's a test of survival.
The temperatures fall to the lowest I've known,
      The icy wind cuts through to the bone.
When we berth our hearts sink low,
      The hatch is not pressed. What a blow.

Rousing the men we sweep once again,
      That arctic wind really gives pain.
At two Christmas Eve morn the hatches is passed,
      Into the warm for some sleep at last.
We've all been up for twenty odd hours,
      We look to the time we can take our showers.
As loading continues we have to shift ship,
      Just get the thing loaded and finish the trip.

All cargo on as daylight breaks,
      Shift to a grab for safety's sakes.
Our hatches now closed we slip to the lock,
      Glad to depart these Antwerp docks.
No pilot on board cap does it all,
      Out at the 'Oost Gat' the mate he'll call.
Steering north-west to the Norfolk coast,
      Anchored off Lynn for that Christmas roast.

Boxing Day morn at the back of five,
      In bound to Kings Lynn we're coming alive.
Sent to a lay-by the *Swan's* on our berth,
      No one for shifting; most crew's gone to earth.
Our captain will shift her, then us too,
      Now we are settled with no more to do.
Off to the pub for some late Christmas cheer,
      Downing a pint of good British beer.

Discharging on Friday finished by dark,
      To wash out now would be a lark.
Washing on Saturday to sail after tea,
      Passage to Rotterdam, then out on a spree.
So bitter the cold no one will play,
      I'll have to celebrate another day.
Off down the road the streets are a-slide,
      To a couple of haunts, deserted inside.

Loading on Monday. Ex lash barge for Calais,
> Time enough, but we don't want to dally.
A two-hour wait for the transit papers,
> On New Years Eve what will be our capers?
Out to the schisms in a north-east seven.
> The inshore traffic zone's shelter is heaven.
Twisting and turning through the Flemish banks,
> Contemplating our New Year pranks.

Unable to anchor at Calais's approach,
> Sought shelter to east but ferries encroached.
Back to the west and stem the seas,
> Ice coats the deck in this freezing breeze.
Just after two the pilot's on board,
> In through the gates and great concord.
All secured for the last time this year,
> Off to the bars and sample the beers.

Out to the centre for old year's night,
> My, how that arctic wind does bite.
Back to a bar close to the ship,
> As locals set crackers, back on board I nip.
Returned with a couple of rocket packs,
> To welcome in the New Year's cracks.
Back to the ship in arctic airs,
> We start the year without our cares.

Nevil

Laurel (New Year)

On New Year's eve we berthed at Calais,
    Once alongside we did not dally.
    Straight to our favourite Cafe Au Retour Du Ferry,
    There we started making merry.
Back to the ship for an evening meal,
    Off up the town; the cold's unreal.
Stopped at the Liverpool first orders that night,
    Then to the Irish bar as the cold does bite.

In the warmth of this bar a guy starts to flirt,
    Showing his knickers under a Ra Ra skirt.
Then to an English pub in the centre of town,
    Back to the ferry bar the cold gets us down.
Seeing in the New Year it's no big thing,
    Not even 'Auld Lang Syne' did they sing.
Firing some rockets excited the French,
    I'd much sooner be with an Islay wench.

New Year's Day we went for a jar,
    In the bitter cold not straying far.
No work on Thursday the factory closed,
    Opened up Friday. The crane driver dozed.
Saturday Sunday no work; it's weekend,
    We don't finish Monday, I'll go round the bend.
Still cargo left on Tuesday night,
    Wednesday's completion brought us delight.

Sailing in daylight for Sidmar Ghent,
    Steel coils and packets to Sutton Bridge sent.
Loaded on Thursday departing that eve,
    Electrical problems forbid us to leave.
As far as the East quay and secured for repair,
    Down to the mission the evening was fair.
On Friday morn the repair I've complete,
    Sailing for Sutton Bridge the crossing is sweet.

A few hours anchored then up on the tide,
　　　　Sad news that Tom, the electrician, has died.
Shane and Ken arrive from Goole,
　　　　Strip down the Lister, there's been a fool.
Off to the Bridge for my first pint of bitter.
　　　　Tim's to change ships; we think he looks fitter.
Back to the ship I'm straight to my bunk,
　　　　The others stayed chatting; they got nearly drunk.

Sunday's dawn and the *Tern* lies astern,
　　　　As I chat to the mate he shows great concern.
Watching their telly for Country File,
　　　　About the *Sea Empress*, the wildlife's defile.
Up to the bar for a lunch time wet,
　　　　The mate off the *Stridence* seems in a fret.
Sunday's on board it's chicken for tea,
　　　　I take a nap then Coro' Street see.

Out for a stroll I see the new mate,
　　　　He gave no idea that to join us he'd hate.
Up to the pub and Tim breaks the news,
　　　　When I ring Tom he's well into snooze.
Apparently I told him how Edd makes a din,
　　　　Next thing we know he's taxied to Lynn.
Nothing can be done till Monday morn,
　　　　Pulling the hatches well before dawn.

All cargo is out well before noon,
　　　　We sit on the mud to sail in the moon.
Gordon Walker joins just till Lynn,
　　　　A favour for Tom he says with a grin.
Opened the hatch Tuesday at seven,
　　　　She's drying well by half eleven.
Alas, once more we cannot please,
　　　　To dry the patch aft we've been on knees.

To blast the piece dry we hire a flame gun,
　　　　I know the sailors had some fun.
Round and round with this huge toasting fork,
　　　　Back and forth the sealing they walk.
Closing the hatches last light of day,
　　　　Off to a pub their usual way.
I'm ashore late to the Park View Hotel,
　　　　Retelling experiences; time went well.

Wednesday pre-dawn the hatch is accepted,
From pipe and belt the cargo recepted.
Pouring their grains all day is a must,
The acres around are covered in dust.
A targeted inspection by the MSA,
Apart from minor things, all's OK.
The cargo loaded by seventeen hundred,
Will there be fog the captain wondered.

Geoffrey Richardson joins us as mate,
I thought with the fog that he'd be late.
Twenty-one thirty the pilot's on board,
The fog so thick it could be sawed.
Navigating the river with the highest of skill,
Gives them both a professional thrill.
Dropping the pilot at the three alpha buoy,
The greatest of vigilance cap will deploy.

Not until near the North East Cross Sands,
Is he relieved from these great demands.
Across the sea and in at the Hook,
John's off home; he's been the cook.
Up to the Park Quay for us to lay-by,
The silo is full that is why.
Now we're ordered for Monday discharge,
Constantly roused by a passing barge.

The long weekend whiled away,
The *Lady Else* also lay.
To and fro the Metro Bar,
All in all we didn't stray far.
Monday morning at five o' clock,
To Souffle's berth Wilhamina Dock.
The belts breaks down but discharge's complete,
Shifted to Vlaadingen a little deplete.

There we've to lie for a couple of days,
The barge with the cargo's in iced waterways.
Wednesday morn and he's made it through,
Coils of reinforcing for a Barking view.
Sailing that eve on a falling tide,
A delightful passage; we're secured alongside.
There's no pleasing one in the office,
No labour laid on despite my profice.
No point in denying, I feel quite flat,
So a Friday discharge and ovies on Sat.

Discharge completed as the fog comes thick,
    Lucky a break as we depart slick.
Out as far as the Mild Blyth buoy,
    Anchored there was not a joy.
Pilot on board Sunday afternoon.
    The mooring gang strained to position us soon.
Once again at Acorn Yard,
    Malcolm's looking ever more tarred.

What's left of Sunday I take a walk,
    Eddy had cooked us the last piece of pork.
Tommy called round but he didn't see me,
    I was ashore having a wet before tea.
By Monday eve we're all on the go,
    The crew's being replaced by Filipino.
Once again my duty's complete,
    I'm off to the island where dreams are sweet.

An overnight drive in a hired car,
    Packed to the gunwales with booty from far.
A ferry across to drop off the load,
    Returning the car to an airport road.
The afternoon flight wings me to you,
    You're locked in my heart; our love shall be true.
For six long weeks I'm free from the sea,
    Just being with you is enough for me.

Nevil

The August moon

The August moon started rising,
In clear twilight sky.
It started off as crimson,
Turning gold as it climbed high.
Every ship and shore light,
Twinkled from near and far.
How magnificent your ascendance,
Accompanied by your star.
My eyes transfixed upon you,
My heart did beat out loud.
I recall the last time,
That you shone out so proud.
Fate brought me to that island,
But you did change my life.
Not coloured crimson, gold, but silver,
Your frost cut like a knife.
That night I met a lady,
Who brought me back to pride.
This woman is devoted,
She's always by my side.

Calum McK

To watch a ferry sail

We stole round the back of a transit shed,
    There in the shadows being caught we dread.
    Watching the industry of a mini cruise,
    This one to sail for the port of Zeebrugge.
The magnificent sight of a North Sea ferry,
    Entertainers on board to make you merry.
As the last of the vehicles are shuffled on board,
    Drivers respond to a mate's co-ord.
He now walks the quay to note the draft,
    The sea door is closed securely aft.
Ping-pong, the speakers are heard from the shore,
    The safety announcements are not to ignore.
Ping-pong, ping-pong the speakers are cursed,
    Sittings for dinner only families are first.
Looking aloft great scanners rotate,
    Feeding the radar an aid for the mate.
In the vast wheelhouse darkened for night,
    They prepare for passage in the dimmest of light.
The nav' lights are burning for others to see,
    Through the huge windows they're dining with glee.

Two plumes of smoke as main engines start,
        Crews called to stations the ship's to depart.
Out on the bridge wing the captain commands,
        Thrusters and engines wait his demands.
Forward and aft they slacken the ropes,
        Out on a dolphin the boatman copes.
Slowly that city moves off its berth,
        Some of the passengers pray for dry earth.
Slewing and backing to line up the locks,
        Most of the ladies are changing to frocks.
Over ten thousand tonnes of magnificent splendour,
        The lock pit clearance is ever so slender.
We're on the move and drive round the dock,
        To watch this wonder slip through the locks.
Nudged into place by the skill of the crew,
        Everyone knows the job they've to do.
The inner gate closed for sluicing ops,
        Till the outer gate opens he feathers the props.
The captain will call to VTS Humber,
        They make a broadcast so there's no blunder.
Out of the piers and into the tide,
        The passengers don't notice; not those inside.
Clear to the sea at the safest of speed,
        Then to Zeebrugge with the greatest of steed.

Calum McK

To join a ship

On an early ferry we left our isle,
  The journey to Garston's many a mile.
This trip for business and for pleasure,
  A chance to see some maritime treasure
By loch and through glens the engine purred,
  Magnificent tranquil vistas for the early bird.
First stop Glasgow to fuel the jeep,
  Buoyed by the beauty not missing our sleep.

South to the borders, how scenic the views,
  First sun of the spring has shifted our blues.
Side many a field where battles were fought,
  Lockerbie's passed with a moment of thought.
First glimpse of the sea as Gretna slips by,
  The hills forming Skiddaw show well in the sky.
With Pennines to left and the Lakes to the right,
  The road over Shap's a stunning sight.

Stopping once more for a snack and some gas,
  Now the accent's of a Lancashire lass.
Through the Forest of Bowland the road snakes south,
  To the industrial belts and the Mersey's mouth.
Straight to the agent at Western we see,
  We're booked in a hotel called Campanile.
Newly constructed by a French group it seems,
  Gaining renown for its excellent cuisine.

A walk before supper as all day we have sat,
        Down to the Mersey and take off some fat.
Side the Manchester canal to Runcorn Dock,
        Our heritage trail blocked by fencing and locks.
The third route we take it brings us quite near,
        The *Arklow Viking* behind fencing we fear.
Round the spiked fence was quite a feat,
        On board for a visit; she really is neat.

Back we walk for a shower and meal,
        After a feast it's tired we feel
Straight to sleep with thoughts of the morrow,
        At the Maritime Museum we'll see some horror.
Beautifully restored but too much for one day,
        In afternoon sun we're Northwich way.
Anderton's the place of the historic boat lift,
        Stripped for restoration this must be our gift.

Our meal this night was really a treat,
        From a fish and chip cafe set out so neat.
Haddock and chips, tea bread and butter.
        So fine there's no words we could utter.
Back to the hotel and out on a spree,
        Doing what sailors have for a century
Enjoying the hospitality of this local bar,
        Just the thing when home is afar.

Our last day together, and oh, what a start,
        Bright springtime sun for our early depart.
The Weavers' Marsh Lock, our first point of call,
        An hour we stayed taking stock of it all.
To Ellsmere Port and the Boat Museum,
        A seven-acre site no time for to see'um.
Then Eastham Ferry for a spot of lunch.
        A tug passed by as a sandwich we munch.

Next place we stop for the Mersey Ferry,
>A round trip we take; most people are merry.
Happy to be on this heritage cruise,
>At Liverpool landing stage our feet feel the blues.
We've walked ourselves out so into a cab,
>To the cathedral we go, it's really quite fab.
An ordination of lay preachers been held,
>The stained glass magnificent, not even a weld.

Now back to ferry to finish our ride,
>New Brighton a place once full of pride.
Looking to sea I'm sure it's the *Larch*,
>Returning to Runcorn my throat feels like parch.
Our last night together the meal is quite light,
>The conversation turns most polite.
Quiet our mood as we watch the TV,
>Enjoying the peace of our own company.

Sunday morn we're speeding along,
>Down to the *Larch* berthed at Garston.
Jack Medherst the captain I'm to relieve,
>Old colleagues are we, but I'll need a good brief.
Some shopping at Asda then back to the ship,
>The crew are preparing for a long ballast trip.
Our last moments together we take Jack to his train,
>'Goodbyes' are at Lime Street; my heart is in pain.

Calum McK

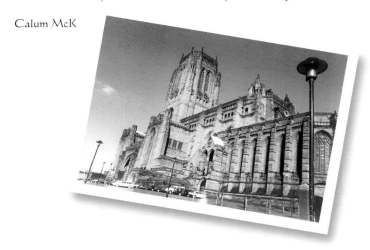

Octofad Wedding

At the ancient farm of Octofad they're making things real grand.
The beasts and fields look better than any in this land.
There is a special reason though things are usual this way,
Patricia the farmer's daughter, it is her wedding day.

Margeret, that's her mother, has worked for a long long while,
To get things in good order and show the best of style.
This working farm looks magnificent as you drive through Nerabus,
You can't get things to look this good without a bit of fuss.

On Thursday there's a gathering for ladies to attend,
A viewing of the presents from many a distant friend.
Friday the ancient custom, of going on a walk,
Round the local villages with many people talk.

Saturday of the wedding there's early morning rain,
We ask the lord for sunshine, surely that's not vain.
The groom he's gone fishing from Bruichladdich pier,
So resplendent at church though, he'll cause a tear.

Afternoon skies are changing, through grey to bright blue,
From the stone church portal, what an outstanding view.
Over the magnificent Loch Indaal and across towards the Oa,
With the north coast of Ireland just beginning to show.

Last guests are being ushered into crowded seats,
It's the kilt that's tradition with neatly pressed pleats.
With the ladies dress in fashion, the vogue's finest style,
Large hats from the mainland to brighten this isle.

The organist plays *Nocturne* as we await the bride,
Faint lilt of the pipes come from outside.
Along the stone path to the open church doors,
On the arm of her father to the man she adores.

She walks down the aisle in her gown of light cream,
Three lovely young bridesmaids attend like a queen.
The groom he strains for a glimpse of his bride,
Before the first hymn, dad leaves her side.

'All things bright and beautiful' they then make their vow,
'I do', said so clearly they're man and wife now.
After the Aaronic blessing some scriptures are read,
The hymn 'Love Divine' makes them really feel wed.

They process from church to 'Praise my soul',
     All have prayed for their bountiful bowl.
Into the church grounds for the photo call,
     As guests start slipping to the Rinns Hall.

Outside this hall guests mill in a crowd,
     Till the bride and her party welcomed us proud.
In afternoon sun there's plenty to drink,
     Beer, wines and whiskies we're invited to sink.

Inside the hall it's set out real neat,
     Two hundred and fifteen, to be fed a great treat.
The top table ready as the couple's piped through,
     A dram for the piper in tradition that's true.

The minister speaks our Saviour's grace,
     Soup is served in little space.
Table by table we're served at the buffet,
     Even the children are not getting huffy.

Salad, quiche, salmon, with beef, chicken and pork,
     This magnificent feast is the centre of talk.
Clarets and wines on the table too,
     Champagne is abundant for the toasting we do.

The speeches over, the tables are pushed back,
     It's on with the ceilidh and really good crack.
Just before two it's brought to an end,
     Everyone's been the best of friend.

Our hosts are thanked for wonderful times,
     We're saying goodbyes after two o clock chimes.
The bride and groom to their honeymoon nest,
     We wish them both the very, very best.

Calum McK

A joke from Edd (The cartoonist)

Two Liverpool sailors are sharing the same cabin.
The first one is writing home to his mother.
After a long period of obvious deep thinking,
He turns to his pal and asks:
'How do you spell *wadal?*'
His pal looked a little perplexed asking:
'*Wadal*, what do you mean wadal?'
'I'm writing to my mum, for her to send
me a pair of wellies wadal fit me,' said the first.
'You are stupid,' said his pal,
'What did they teach you at school? It's not *wadal*, you fool,
It's dadal fit you.'

Edward Kirkbride

Larch

Nine o' clock Sunday the ninth of March,
That's when I stepped aboard the *Larch*.
At Garston Dock she looked real neat,
To cover on this should be be a treat.
I'm relieving a colleague all know as Jack,
Captain Medherst his name; we go right back.
There's Ian Cunneen. We sailed on the *Finch*,
This stint could be a bit of a synch.

Carol was cook but she's to go home,
Harry due back he's cause for a groan.
The galley and mess, not clean as he'd left,
She said it was down to a guy on the theft.
Phil the mate is journeying too,
George from Kings Lynn is coming through.
Peter the second mate's staying on board,
All seems set for a real good accord.
Last not least is Joao the deckhand,
The oldest on board and far from his land.

Discharged on Sunday is a little unkind,
Sailing in ballasts, a bit of a bind.
Victualling the ship from Asda store,
Some consider this quite a chore.
We drive Jack to Lime Street station,
Where sailors have left for many a generation.
Now is the time for my girl to depart,
She's to drive north; she'll carry my heart.

A mini tour of Liverpool's centre,
With Ian a sample of pubs I enter.
Returning to ship mid afternoon,
Washing the hold, the lights are a boon.
After tea I watch the Street,
A walk up to Garston a last minute treat.
At twenty-two hundred the pilot is due,
The damned bloody fog as thick as a stew.

Thick as a bag when we slip our last rope,
Slow as a snail to the lock pit we grope.
Then when the tide has eased to slow,
The ropes are cast and off we go.
Outward bound with the fo'c's'le unseen,
Clear visibility by the buoy called Queen.
The pilot's away at the outer station,
Our course set west for the Skerries' separation.

Cap's call to office on Monday morn.
There's no denying we're quite forlorn.
A ballast trip to Amsterdam Port,
Loading at Amferts is usually fraught.
Round Land's End and up the Channel,
A short on the kettle throws a panel.
Patchy fog as we wend our way,
Boarding our pilot Thursday midday.

Astern The Willow we had to wait,
Alex Jax's the skipper, but I see the mate.
Once under the loader I'm off to the town,
Ian is with me to a street most renown.
The taxi's too late, so step on the bus,
Then on a train, it causes no fuss.
A few minutes ride and we're at the centre,
Then into a shop that's dark as you enter.

Back to Sloterdyke by separate trains,
On the same bus without any strains.
Loading continues during the night,
Pete slips to the mish for a pint of the light.
Early Saturday securing for sea,
Clearing the locks it's tired we be.
As evening falls there's British TV,
I'm wishing to hell that you were with me.

South-west the course all of Sunday,
The fog's quite thick at dawn on Monday.
There's no chance of the Channel Du Fore,
So it's into the Ushant separation law.
Out clear the rocks of the Raz der Sein,
We can see the horizon again.
Now south-east past the Ile de Yeu,
Calling the agent for the pilot's view.

Past the Ile de Axe we board our pilot,
He and the captain almost riot.
The tide now low she's sniffed the ground,
Steering like a bitch till deep water's found.
Flood tide now so swing off the locks,
What a struggle to enter those docks.
Securing safely starboard side too,
Off to our beds with no more to do.

At eight on Wednesday the crane swings slow,
The agent is telling a tale of woe.
Afternoon figures show better discharge,
After our tea in the town we're at large.
To a couple of bars then back to the ship,
Quiet as mice to our bunks we slip.
Thursday dawns sunny and bright,
Making the hold wash quite a delight.

Pilot on board at half past eleven,
Passage north a gift from heaven.
Washing the hold in springtime sun,
At San Nazair we've no time for fun.
Commencing the load well before dawn,
Come afternoon tide we're full of corn.
A pilot on board as the ebb tide's away,
Clear of the channel after a long, long day.

Inside Bell Isle the course north-west.
Dawn is breaking as we come near to Brest.
Through the Pass du Sain and the Channel du Four,
Ushant control's not the usual bore.
Clearing this light north-easterly we head.
Three hundred miles to the place we dread.
East of the Varne we must cross the lanes,
To abide by the rules we take great pains.

Passage north was quite a pleasure,
Into the Humber short time for leisure.
Discharging the ship till ten at night,
Continuing Wednesday from very first light.
Ian Cunneen's on leave at Goole,
John Atkinson's back he's starred at school.
Visitors from Hull, and then from York,
All in all lots of family talk.

A call to Shaen a last minute hitch,
No fresh water it's the pressure switch.
With the tug boat, *Viking*, pulling our head,
Back through the bridgeway clearing the shed.
Seventeen metres under this canopy.
Thirteen metres out from the quay.
Who passed these plans must be a fool,
Blocking the passage to Barge Dock Goole.

Swept past Spurn on an ebbing tide,
My, how we were in for a bumpy ride.
Flat calm seas till we pass North Hinder,
Time for me to call my kinder.
Then mounting seas from a westerly gale,
All of the crew feel a little frail.
Embarking a pilot at Flushing Roads,
Through to Antwerp for our fertiliser loads.

Loading the cargo by night and day,
Good Friday morning we're back under way.
Down the Schelt and away to the west,
The weather behaving its very best.
Beautifully clear sky at night,
The comet makes a breathtaking sight.
Easter Monday Land's End we pass,
Late that night at anchor alas.

Twenty-four hours at Cheek Point we lay,
Then to Stokestown discharged in a day.
Arrived and sailed in the middle of night,
Sailing south for Teignmouth's delight.
Arriving there Friday's morn,
Once again we're loading at dawn.
Completion too late for the afternoon tide,
A night on the town we need no guide.

Ian pays a visit he comes with a girl.
Heide her name, she causes a whirl.
Off to Malloy's, join the rest of the crew,
Then to some more enjoying the view.
Into my bunk around midnight,
Up for the pilot before daylight.
A two-day passage in moderate seas,
Westerly winds give a refreshing breeze.

Boarding our pilot at the Maas Centre station,
News that a bridge is non operation.
Securing at Dordrecht's Handles quay,
So shippers and agents have time to agree.
An alternative place to discharge this clay,
Successfully completed in the same day.
Off down the Maas after washing our hold,
Once again long hours unfold.

No loading this night, start Tuesday's eve,
Load through darkness; Wednesday we leave.
A beautiful day the best of the year,
An occupied berth is now what we fear.
Shall we lie to an anchor? Or go straight on?
I sit in my cabin waiting the agent's deliberation.
Thursday morn at the pilot station,
First to the wall then a berth adjacent.

News that Jack will travel tomorrow,
I pack my bags with the deepest of sorrow.
I will travel to Kent and pick up the *Swan*,
I'll miss the lads when I've gone.
So off on a train to Ramsgate Harbour,
On the Silver Lad I'll go no farther.
Than to the Swan anchored off,
Relieving Chris Reynolds; he's quite a toff.

Nevil

To give my captain a hand

T here's a small piece of waterway inside Ternuzen's East lock,
    Not more than a half mile long; it's end is in a block.
The bargees use it for getting their sleep,
When you walk by you don't hear a peep.
    Only the sound as water laps,
Once in a while a halliard fraps.
    Such was the state not a sound from the land,
The night I gave my captain a hand.

I was a lad on an outbound coaster,
    What a day; it had been a roaster.
How in the black of that summer's night,
    Sound could be heard even though slight.
The captain he'd sailed no pilot on board,
    Called to the East Locks by Ternuzen co-ord.
I'm on the afterdeck by the breeze being fanned,
    The night I gave my captain a hand.

'The East Locks my lad, have you passed through?'
    'Yes indeed at least a good few.'
I lied of course I'd been just the once,
    But in front of my mates I'd look such a ponce.
'Then stand inside and you steer the way,
    My eyes are tired it's been a long, long day.'
My chest sprang out my voice made bland,
    The night I gave my captain a hand.

'Take the channel to starboard and keep to the side.'
    How I hoped he'd not find I'd lied.
Things were good as the main channel is cleared,
    The captain's confident as to starboard I steered.
This confidence alas was not to last long.
    As he sensed that things were wrong.
No way was this the way he'd planned,
    The night I gave my captain a hand.

A black abyss before us lay,
    The captain looks with great dismay.
'Where are those signals to enter safe?'
    'Just round the corner cap, have faith.'

Now craft were moored on either side,
　　The channel left open not all that wide.
Should they be there those piles of sand?
　　The night I gave my captain a hand.

Dead slow to starboard we still swing,
　　Damn and blast it, cap can't see a thing.
Then in the loom of an odd street light,
　　The end of the channel came into sight.
Shouts from the master as the ship thrusts astern,
　　This is one lesson that I would learn.
To have told the truth and not be so grand,
　　The night I gave my captain a hand

I remember the dogs, as they started to bark.
　　Oh, my goodness, what a lark.
Seems every breed from under the sun,
　　How they thought that this was great fun.
With the engines roaring from ahead to astern,
　　The children are wakening to parents' concern.
The captain swears that he's been damned,
　　The night I gave my captain a hand.

The captain's instructions now being perplexed,
　　The bargees are shouting abuse from their decks.
The children cry out, as the dogs bark and holla,
　　Back down the channel that ship did follow.
A whole floating town brought close to a riot,
　　How that captain wanted a pilot.
All accused him of being canned,
　　The night I gave my captain a hand.

The mate back aft gives blunt advice,
　　He'd change the master at any price.
Even the cook is out of bed,
　　In just a towel and the barest of thread.
As I look around there's nothing I can do,
　　Say 'There you are, cap, it's over to you.'
I'm sure he vowed to resign command,
　　The night I gave my captain a hand.

Calum McK

To lose a pal

It really was a sad, sad day,
    When Tom told me that Tim had passed away.
Our lives had started poles apart,
But what a fellow, what a heart.
He'd been a boarder at a public school,
While I was the product of a council's rule.

He apprenticed in the fleet BP,
Me at an aircraft factory making tea.
Then an officer in China Nav,
With style and bearing others wished they had.
Tim worked ashore in the Middle East,
Tells the story of a damned great beast.
A Saluki or hunting dog,
And how he'd take it for a jog.
To the desert in the back of his car,
Then pushed out as Tim's off far.
Keeping up with his 'E' type Jag,
He's sure that dog was sired by a nag.

His favoured place being Hong Kong,
To return to these parts he would long.
He gained accord with the diplomatic corps,
The life he led was not a bore.
In New Zealand he settled and took to his heart,
Alas he and his wife they would part.
Engaged as a mate on a Ro-Ro ferry,
He'd have made an excellent equerry.

Tim returned to his place in the UK,
I don't know why he never did say.
New Zealand's loss most surely my gain,
When he joined the *Maple* running to Spain.
In no times at all we'd jelled as a team,
From Russia to Portugal we could never disclose,
Some of the places we've been 'Mon Repose'.

Tim was a guy that always had talk,
One thing though he'd never walk.
A night in Dublin we're out for a jar,
Then onwards late to a Theatre Bar.

Now early morn and the revellers thick,
To catch a taxi you had to be slick.
Tim slipped off I didn't see where,
He's back with transport to match his flair.
Shining black and drawn by horse,
Through the centre of Dublin he'd lay the course.
Off to some wine bar and drink our toast,
He really was a magnificent host.

After my misdemeanour, we had to part.
I'd made a trip without a good chart.
If he'd been there my nose would be clean,
We'd have cleared those rocks, he'd have seen.
We sailed together just twice more,
In Selby town our heads were sore.
Then on the *Laurel* at Christmas time,
The bitterest cold it was a crime.

At Sutton Bridge we said farewell,
We planned to meet and give it hell.
But alas we'll sail no more.
Not till I'm at that pearly door.
You'll be in, I'm sure of that.
Come and give my back a pat
For now my friend we're to be apart,
We'll take a drink to your good heart.
We'll bow our heads and talk in sorrow,
We wish you best, and a new tomorrow.

Calum McK